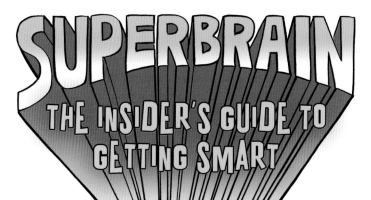

SUPERBRAIN

THE INSIDER'S GUIDE TO GETTING SMART

Toronto Public Library
Art by Dave Whamond

annick press
toronto + new york + vancouver

We acknowledge the support of the Canada Council for the Arts, the Ontario Arts Council, and the Government of Canada through the Canada Book Fund (CBF) for our publishing activities.

ONTARIO ARTS COUNCIL
CONSEIL DES ARTS DE L'ONTARIO
an Ontario government agency
un organisme du gouvernement de l'Ontario

Cataloging in Publication
     Superbrain : the insider's guide to getting smart / Toronto
Public Library ; illustrated by Dave Whamond.

Includes bibliographical references.
ISBN 978-1-55451-734-3 (pbk.).–ISBN 978-1-55451-735-0 (bound).–
ISBN 978-1-55451-736-7 (html).–ISBN 978-1-55451-737-4 (pdf)

Study skills–Juvenile literature. 2. Learning–Juvenile literature. I. Whamond, Dave, illustrator II. Toronto Public Library, author III. Title: Super brain.

LB1601.S87 2015   j371.30281   C2014-905950-7
                                             C2014-905951-5

Distributed in Canada by:
Firefly Books Ltd.
50 Staples Avenue, Unit 1
Richmond Hill, ON L4B 0A7
Published in the U.S.A. by Annick Press (U.S.) Ltd.

Distributed in the U.S.A. by:
Firefly Books (U.S.) Inc.
P.O. Box 1338
Ellicott Station
Buffalo, NY 14205

Printed in China

Visit us at: www.annickpress.com

Also available in e-book format. Please visit www.annickpress.com/ebooks.html for more details. Or scan

Table of Contents

What is a library?

A library is many different things to different people. Some people think it's a place that has thousands of books on thousands of different topics that you can borrow and read at any time. And that's true. But the library is much more than that.

The library is also a place where people from all kinds of communities gather to talk and share ideas. It's a place where you can participate in different activities and events. It's a place where you can borrow movies or magazines or graphic novels. It's a place that's staffed with people who want to help you explore new things. The library is also a "virtual" place that you can visit on the web to download e-books, stream music, and more.

In other words, the library is a place of superpower intelligence, giving you an endless supply of adventure, knowledge, and fun. Best of all? With your library card, you have access to it all!

In Toronto Public Library's *Superbrain: The Insider's Guide to Getting Smart,* we show you how to get your super brain working at full speed both inside and outside of school, while making the best use of your library. In each chapter, we give you tips on how to get organized, how to research topics, how to use the web, how you can find your learning style, and how to understand different types of leaders. There's no limit to where you'll go.

There are many adventures waiting for you at your public library. We can't wait to join you on your journey.

Anne Bailey,
Acting City Librarian, Toronto Public Library
October 2014

Chapter 1

PREPARE YOUR LAIR
CALLING ALL SUPERHEROES

Ever wanted to be a superhero? Superheroes have to be ready to learn new things, their whole life long. Learning is the superpower they all share, and it can be yours too! This book will show you how.

Maybe you can't fly (at least not without a plane). And you haven't discovered the secret of invisibility (yet!). That car over there? You may not be able to flip it over with one hand, but that doesn't mean you don't have a superpower right at your fingertips—the ability to learn.

But beware of your number one villain—ignorance! Ignorance will try to stop you in your path. Learn to vanquish him!

Lifelong learning is what happens when you use your learning superpowers at every stage in your life. Superheroes have to keep learning when they fight crime and work at day jobs as scientists, reporters, or photographers. Lifelong learners are the superheroes of our time!

Lifelong learning isn't just for superheroes, though. Ordinary people also need to find information for all sorts of reasons:

* Actors need to research their roles.
* Video game designers have to stay on top of the latest computer systems.
* Athletes can get ahead of the competition by studying their opponents.

Successful learning follows a pattern. Good learners need to

* recognize *when* they need information,
* identify the *kind* of information they need,
* *find* the information and *judge its quality*,
* *organize* it, and
* *use* it to solve the problem at hand.

Information isn't just used to answer questions on a test. It's used for *many* different reasons. Think about how you use different kinds of information in your own life:

* reading a bus schedule to plan a trip
* listening to the weather forecast before deciding what to wear
* comparing prices when choosing a snack at the grocery store

Learning how to learn is a skill that you'll use throughout your life, time and time again.

WHAT IF I DON'T FEEL LIKE LEARNING?

If you've ever felt unmotivated to learn something, maybe the task at hand didn't seem important to you. But even if learning feels like a chore, it's a great opportunity to hone your superpowers, like super-intelligence!

No matter what you set out to learn, treat it like a challenge. Remember the fun you had solving a puzzle or doing a scavenger hunt? If things like this excite you, then trust us: you can have fun about learning anything (yes, even the multiplication tables!).

In order to learn something new, you need to find a way to make the learning meaningful to you. You need to want to do something in order to do it well, so ask yourself this question: How does the task at hand fit into my goals and dreams?

☆ Want to become a better skateboarder? Understanding the basic laws of physics can help you master that tricky ollie.
☆ Want to create a cool website that showcases your photography? The more you know about technology, the better your site will be, and the better your pictures will look!
☆ Interested in putting up buildings? Want to become a builder or an engineer? You'll need to know about math to ensure that your buildings actually stay up!

Poetic Numbers:
Super-Learner Daniel Tammet

Daniel Tammet has a strange superpower: he sees beautiful colors and emotions in numbers. Daniel has synesthesia, which means that he sees words and numbers as colors and shapes.

Pi is the world's longest number. It is made up of trillions upon trillions of digits, but is usually shortened to 3.14. When most people look at the number pi, they see infinite digits with no obvious pattern. Daniel sees something else.

He holds the European record for pi recitation. When he was 25 years old, he recited 22,514 digits of pi, which took 5 hours and 9 minutes!

How was he able to do that? According to him, he had to first invent meaning before being able to memorize such a long number. For Daniel, reciting pi was like describing the patterns of shapes and colors that he was seeing, so he treated the task as though he were telling a story.

Daniel's unique case can inspire you to find patterns in anything. The trick to learning is to make those patterns meaningful to you.

What does success look like to you? This is a tough question. The answer is likely to change throughout your life. But no matter how old you are, you can always

☆ weigh your strengths and interests, and consider the ways you learn best. (Don't know the answer to that? Take the quiz on page 9 and find out.)

☆ get to know yourself and what makes you happy. You'll be better able to judge how you might feel fulfilled now and in the future.

☆ remember that success comes in lots of forms. Not everyone needs to be a millionaire. If you love working with animals, completing a veterinary technician diploma will probably make you happier than trying to follow in Bill Gates's footsteps.

FIND YOUR LEARNING STYLE

Visual learners learn by seeing. Auditory learners learn by listening. Kinesthetic learners learn by doing. What kind of learner are you? Take this quiz and find out!

Q1 Where do you prefer to sit in class?
a) I don't care where I sit, so long as I can hear what's going on.
b) I like to sit at the front of the classroom.
c) I like to sit at the back of the classroom where there's more room, near the door.
Answer: *a) auditory learner b) visual learner c) kinesthetic learner*

Q2 What's your preferred working style?
a) Listening to music helps me work and concentrate.
b) I prefer to work in silence.
c) When I work, I like to move around; walking helps me think more clearly.
Answer: *a) auditory learner b) visual learner c) kinesthetic learner*

Q3 If you had to give a presentation in class, what would you do?
c) Moderate a class discussion.
a) Create a killer PowerPoint presentation.
b) Lead a group activity to teach the class.
Answer: *a) auditory learner b) visual learner c) kinesthetic learner*

Q4 If you were to get in trouble in class, what would it be for?

a) talking too much
b) doodling in my textbook
c) fidgeting

Answer: *a) auditory learner*
b) visual learner c) kinesthetic learner

Q5 Which of the following excites you the most?

a) discussing things in class
b) when textbooks include charts and diagrams
c) doing activities in class

Answer: *a) auditory learner b) visual learner*
c) kinesthetic learner

Q6 What's your favorite after-school activity?

a) listening to audio books borrowed from my local library
b) playing video games
c) dancing or playing sports

Answer: *a) auditory learner b) visual learner*
c) kinesthetic learner

It's time to tally up your score! Count how many As, Bs, and Cs you got to find out your strongest learning style. If you got mostly As, you're an auditory learner. If you got mostly Bs, you're a visual learner. If you got mostly Cs, you're a kinesthetic learner

This quiz helps you understand yourself better, and introduces you to new ways of learning. Not everyone is just one type of learner. You might be a strong visual learner, but you also need to move around while learning. Knowing how you learn will help you be successful.

Make the Most of Your Learning Style

Auditory learner: You learn best by reading out loud and respond well to verbal instructions. Amp up your learning by

* paying close attention in class to what your teacher says
* recording yourself reading out loud and playing it back when studying for a test

Visual learner: You learn best by reading books and taking notes. It's easy for you to memorize information if you visualize it first or see it in picture form. Next time that midterm rolls around, try

* using colors to highlight similar concepts (for example, a blue highlighter for dates, pink for names, and green for definitions)
* making flash cards to help you memorize facts and vocabulary

Kinesthetic learner: You like being active and communicate physically. To get straight As this semester, consider

* riding an exercise bike while reading your study notes. Keep that brain (and body) of yours going!
* putting action figures on a map and moving them around to study important moments in history. Role playing anyone?

No two superheroes share the same superpowers! Don't become frustrated if one approach isn't working. There isn't a single right or wrong way to learn, just different approaches.

YOUR NOT-SO-SECRET LAIR

Every good superhero has a secret headquarters. The base of operations for super-learners like you is the library. In the library, you can arm yourself with information for whatever task you put your mind to. It might not be the batcave, but it's still powerful.

The library is a safe and free resource. You'll find librarians there who care about your learning and who want to help you succeed. Find your nearest public library and start exploring.

How to Use the Library

Libraries are about more than just books and research. With movies, magazines, music, comics, graphic novels, computers, books, games, 3-D printers, and so much more, the library is a (not-so-secret) hub of superpower intelligence!

The American Library Association says the library is "the strongest and most far-reaching community resource for lifelong learning." It's here that you'll encounter the joy of discovery, picking out materials that excite you—not just what you need to finish an assignment.

Curious people often make a habit of using the library their whole life long. They've discovered the ultimate secret weapon: that the quest for knowledge is the most thrilling superpower in any hero's arsenal.

But beware: learning adventures may become addictive. Once you start, you may not be able to stop.

Chapter 2

KNOW YOUR MISSION

EVERY SUPERHERO HAS A MISSION

Your mission, should you chose to accept it, is to bust down the walls of learning—KAPOW! Now Learning doesn't have to stop at the end of the school day when the bell rings. So take a deep breath and look around. See the playground? The skate park? Your house? Learning in unexpected places could be the secret superpower you never knew you had.

Whenever and wherever you collect information to answer a question that solves a problem, that's called research. Research can happen in a lot of places.

* Want to settle a bet with your sister? Better do your research! Take to the Internet or an encyclopedia and prove an argument wrong. Turns out Super-Woman DID have a magic lasso!
* Curious about jazz music? Borrow a CD from your local library or use one of their free music-streaming services to have a listen.
* Bike broken and you don't know how to fix it? Can't afford to take it in? Check out a bike repair manual (in print or online) or a video tutorial, and start learning how to fix it yourself.

Research is one of the best ways to sharpen your critical-thinking superpowers, which you will need if you want to be a super-learner your whole life long. (See Chapter 3 for more about critical thinking.)

BREAK IT DOWN: THE RESEARCH PROCESS

SUIT UP! GET YOUR BRAINSTORMING CAPE ON

Before any adventure, superheroes always suit up: a cape to help them leap over tall buildings, a utility belt stocked with gadgets to fight villains, and a mask to hide their secret identity.

You may not have a power ring, an indestructible shield, or a freeze gun at your disposal, but you need to suit up all the same. Get your thoughts in order before facing your next learning challenge. Put on that brainstorming cap—er, cape!—and get started with a K-W-L chart.

This chart will help you focus on a topic or task. Begin by creating three columns:

* **K** column: what you **KNOW** about the topic.
* **W** column: what you **WANT** to know.
* **L** column: what you've **LEARNED**.

Before you start your research, fill in the first two columns of a chart like the one above. Look at the skills, experience, and knowledge you've got and use them to reach your goal.

List the places you can look to find the things you want to know in the second column, too: books, magazines, the Internet, the library, etc.

After completing your research, fill in the last column. What have you learned so far? What do you still want to learn? Compare what you've learned to what you thought you knew at the beginning of the process. Question your assumptions and perspectives:

* Has anything changed about what you thought you knew?
* If so, how did it change and why?
* What can you take away from your learning experience?

Fighting for Girls' Rights: Education Advocate Malala Yousafzai

Pakistani schoolgirl Malala Yousafzai is a real fighter. Like all superheroes, she stands up for an important cause—the right to education for girls and women.

In 2009, Malala began writing a blog about life under Taliban rule. The Taliban is a fundamentalist political group known for outlawing education for women. Malala defied the Taliban and continued to attend school, writing publicly about her passion for education. Her bravery earned her an International Children's Peace Prize as well as Pakistan's National Youth Peace Prize. The Taliban saw this as a threat, and decided to take action against her.

In 2012, a Taliban gunman boarded the school bus that Malala was on, and shot her. Malala not only survived this vicious attack—she fought back. The next year, *Time* magazine named her one of the most influential people in the world. She wrote a book about her horrific experiences, and the Malala Fund was established as a charity for the education of girls all around the world.

"I speak—not for myself, but for all girls and boys. I raise up my voice—not so that I can shout, but so that those without a voice can be heard.

> *Those who have fought for their rights:*
> *Their right to live in peace.*
> *Their right to be treated with dignity.*
> *Their right to equality of opportunity.*
> *Their right to be educated."*

—*Part of a speech given by Malala Yousafzai to the United Nations on July 12, 2013*

MASTER MULTIPLE IDENTITIES

Managing a super-identity means first managing your time. Superheroes often live double lives to protect their crime-fighting alter egos. You probably don't have to worry about this, but you do have to manage multiple responsibilities: juggling school work, chores, extracurricular stuff, and time with family and friends.

Superheroes are expert time managers and you can be one, too. (How do you think Superman gets in and out of that phone booth so fast?) Train yourself to use the time you've got by following these steps:

☆ **Get an agenda:** Find one place that works for you where you can track all that stuff that needs to get done. A small notebook, a calendar app on your computer or mobile device, or a large wall poster will work.

☆ **Create your own batcave:** A study or work space that you enjoy using will motivate you to keep learning. Clear away the clutter, organize your work supplies, keep the time in view, and hang up something that inspires you, like a photograph, a favorite quote, or a poster that you really love.

☆ **Get a good meal:** Nutritious food (like fruits, veggies, and yogurt) will keep you feeling your best so that you can achieve whatever you put your mind to.

★ **Get your zzs:** It's impossible to focus on learning when you're exhausted. If you get a good night's sleep, you'll wake up feeling rested and ready for whatever learning challenges may come your way.

★ **Don't forget about fun:** Plan for fun. Build in breaks from working so that you can let your ideas percolate. Sometimes all you need is a little bit of distance between you and your work to have that eureka moment. Take a walk outside, have a dance break, do some baking—anything that will get you to focus on something other than the task at hand for a little while.

WHAT KIND OF LEADER ARE YOU?

Autocratic, democratic, or consensus—which style of leadership do you prefer? Take this quiz and find out!

Q1 You consider yourself a good leader because
a) you place the group's opinions and needs over those of any individual
b) you say so
c) you have lots of experience, which can help guide the group's decisions
Answer: *a) democratic b) autocratic c) consensus*

Q2 What animal best describes you?
a) a mama grizzly bear nurturing, protecting, and guiding her young
b) a lion, the king of the jungle
c) a member of a school of fish
Answer: *a) democratic*
b) autocratic c) consensus

Q3 Which historical figure do you most look up to?
a) Angela Merkel, the Chancellor of Germany
b) Alexander the Great, the world's greatest military leader
c) Martin Luther King, Jr., the American civil rights leader
Answer: *a) democratic*
b) autocratic c) consensus

Q4 When leading a group, you find it's easier to
a) make sure the majority rules
b) tell others what to do
c) turn decisions over to the group
Answer: *a) democratic b) autocratic c) consensus*

Q5 What do you enjoy doing in your free time?
a) participating in the school's debate team
b) bossing your little sister around
c) creating a collaborative art piece or playing on a team
Answer: *a) democratic b) autocratic c) consensus*

Q6 What do you want to be when you get older?
a) a politician
b) a professional football coach
c) a crew member on one of NASA's missions to Mars
Answer: *a) democratic b) autocratic c) consensus*

It's time to tally up your score! If you got mostly As, you're a democratic leader. If you got mostly Bs, you're an autocratic leader. If you got mostly Cs, you're a consensus leader.

Different Ways to Lead

Sometimes the best learning happens when we work together. Working in groups takes leadership, but it's not always easy.

Each leadership style has pros and cons. Just because you scored one way or another on the quiz, don't worry—you're not boxed in. Leadership can change according to the kinds of people you're working with and what you are trying to do together.

Autocratic leaders are in control and give clear directives to the group. This is a helpful style to follow in an emergency situation. Many superheroes use this style when they need to vanquish their enemies.

Democratic leaders let majority opinion rule. This is a very popular leadership style and one that you're probably already familiar with.

Consensus leaders remain neutral as they wait for unanimous agreement. This style can sometimes mean taking a little longer to make decisions, but it may be worth it in the end!

"WITH GREAT POWER COMES GREAT RESPONSIBILITY"

Part of being a lifelong learner is deciding for yourself what questions need answering and what problems need solving. Figuring this out boosts your (super) power, which is fun, and also—like the famous quote says—a lot of responsibility. No one ever said being a superhero was going to be a walk (or leap!) in the park.

If you're preparing to learn because you have to—for a test, or something that's been assigned—it might seem like a waste of time. But when you stop and consider the benefits of learning—like knowing how to calculate fractions when your brother is trying to steal your share of the pizza!—you'll be closer to understanding the real meaning of your super-mission.

By busting down the walls of learning, you're empowering yourself and others to strive for personal success and be good citizens. And isn't doing your best and helping others the best superpower of all?

So suit up and get your game on, because the next chapter brings you face-to-face with your villains. Are you ready?

Chapter 3

TACKLE YOUR VILLAINS

KNOW YOUR ENEMIES

Every superhero has an arch nemesis: it might be an alien, a criminal, or a natural disaster. But for super-learners, false and misleading information are the two true villains to vanquish.

Fortunately, super-learners have a special power: the ability to see many different points of view. This means they can recognize information that is biased from a mile away. Super-learners do more than just listen: They decide for themselves what to accept as useful. They think about facts they may have taken for granted (remember that K-W-L chart? see page 19) and weigh people's motives before accepting anything as truth.

Inadequate factoids are everywhere. That's why super-learners must be on guard and prepared to dig deep into any topic, separating what's false and misleading from the information they know they can trust.

Villains creep up in all sorts of situations. Get ready to defeat them by learning all you can about a subject and asking some tough questions. Think about the following situations:

Bizbot Toy Company says kids like their toys better than the ones their competitor, the Buzibot Toy Company, makes.

☆ Where did the company get its facts? Whose facts might be correct? How do you check them out? What sources can you access to learn more?

Lickety Lou Ice Cream swears their products are the best tasting out there, while their arch enemy, Mr. Freeze Ice Cream, claims to have proven that their ice cream is the tastiest.

☆ How will you decide who is right? What is meant by the word proven? Have any tests been conducted? If so, how were they conducted? Has the company provided any real evidence of people's personal taste preferences?

Read on to get the skills you'll need to understand
☆ how information is **organized**,
☆ how to **find** it, and
☆ how to **evaluate** it.

Together these skills are called "information literacy"—the superpower you need to vanquish your enemies.

X-RAY VISION

Super-learners have an invaluable secret ability: they can sift through things to pinpoint exactly what they're looking for—sort of like Superman's X-ray vision. Maybe you won't be able to see through walls like he does, but you can learn to cultivate your special power of observation—the ability to identify patterns across different types of sources.

If you understand how knowledge is organized, you'll have an easier time locating and evaluating it. Similar to how all stories follow a pattern—with a beginning, a middle, and an end—you'll find a pattern in how information is organized among different types of sources.

The following tools (common to both print and online sources) can help you zero in on what you're looking for:

* a table of contents (print) or a site map (online)
* headings (print) and site menus (online)
* indexes (print) and digital search features (online)
* a glossary or appendix
* pictures and accompanying captions
* charts, tables, and graphs

Another tool that can help you hone your X-ray vision is a *classification scheme*. This is a fancy term for how materials are organized in a library. Think of it as a secret code. Library items are assigned call numbers that tell people where on the shelves the items can be found. Most public libraries around the world use a classification scheme known as the Dewey Decimal System—DDC (Dewey Decimal Classification) for short. Check out the appendix at the back of this book (page 64) for a more detailed look at the DDC. For now, here's a quick breakdown of categories and their assigned numbers:

* 000 general works
* 100 philosophy
* 200 religion
* 300 people and the way they live
* 400 language
* 500 science
* 600 technology
* 700 the arts
* 800 literature
* 900 history

How People Get Information

ON THE HUNT: FINDING WHAT YOU NEED

Once you've found the information you need, you'll have to record it. Sure, superheroes may have high-tech gadgets, trusty sidekicks, and magic powers to help them remember things, but sometimes simple is best. The tools you need for your special assignment can even be found in the common junk drawer …

Recipe Card Mission

Search your home for these rectangular cards where, once upon a time, family recipes were recorded. Can't find any? How about cutting up scrap paper and making your own cards? A regular sheet of paper works, too. The important part is that the information you record can be easily sorted and rearranged into subtopics.

Physical cards not your style? A handful of online apps mimic the same thing:

☆ Mindola SuperNotecard: These digital note cards can be organized online and grouped into categories just like physical note cards can be.

☆ Evernote: Create searchable and sortable tags for each card in this note-taking app.

On to the mission at hand!

Taking Notes

☆ Include one idea or quote per note card. Keep it short and sweet.

☆ Keep track of all sources. This will save you time later—if you need to go back to the original source or when compiling a bibliography. On each card, make sure to record the information below.

    ☆ title
    ☆ page numbers
    ☆ author and/or editor
    ☆ year of publication
    ☆ name of publisher and the city of publication
    ☆ the URL or website address of a webpage

☆ To avoid unintentionally taking credit for someone else's work, use quotation marks around any direct quotes.

☆ Use colored recipe cards to organize your ideas or sections of your research. For example, when doing an American history essay on the Civil War (1861–1865), record information about slavery on blue recipe cards and information about secession on green ones.

Sorting Your Cards

☆ Organizing cards into different piles is a good way to stay on track. If you are writing an essay, create a pile for all the points to be made in the introduction, another one for the points you'll use in the conclusion, and a bunch for each of the paragraphs in between.

☆ Rearrange the cards in each pile to see how your points work best.

Word Wall Mission (The Sticky Kind)

When brainstorming, use sticky notes to create a word wall:

☆ Jot down one main idea per note (a name, a key event, etc.)
☆ Sort each note below a main column.
☆ Let your ideas collide by re-sorting and rearranging your sticky notes in some other way. This will help you come up with new ways of looking at a topic or problem.
☆ While reading, jot down ideas on sticky notes. You can add these to your word wall later.

Digital Bookmark Mission

When doing research online, don't forget to bookmark interesting and useful websites and articles. This will really save you time when you want to go back to them. You can add a bookmark to any web browser. (Not sure what a web browser is? Head on over to the next chapter to take a peek!) Some browsers prefer the term *favorites* over *bookmarks*, but whatever you want to call them, you'll find the option to save sites along the top part of the browser's page.

Accidental Super-Learners: Failure Is Not the Enemy

Sometimes great things happen by accident. You may set out to prove one thing and end up discovering something completely different. You never know where learning will take you.

Alexander Fleming, Scientist

Next time you go on vacation, here's a thought: don't clean your room—it could save lives! After returning from vacation in 1928, Fleming found mold on one of the petri dishes in his lab. He was surprised to see that the mold had dissolved all of the bacteria around it. Turns out there was a powerful substance in this unintended mold that prevented bacteria from growing. Fleming later named his discovery penicillin, which became a drug used to fight infection. It has saved countless lives to this very day.

Ruth G. Wakefield, Innkeeper

As the co-owner of an inn, Ruth had her hands full making meals for her guests. One day, determined to bake cookies for dessert, she was upset to find that she'd run out of baking chocolate. Instead, she cut up pieces of a semisweet chocolate bar, adding them to her dough,

thinking they'd blend in. But they didn't. They kept their chip form instead, giving the world the greatest baking mistake of all time: the chocolate chip cookie.

Richard James, Engineer

Richard James was working hard to create a spring that could hold a ship's equipment in rough waters—a very serious task. Then something not-so-serious happened: his "invention" accidentally fell on the floor, jiggling in a funny way. After experimenting with different  types of steel wire, Mr. James was able to make his discovery "walk," creating one of the most popular toys ever sold. His wife named his accidental creation Slinky and the rest, as they say, was history. Slinky doesn't just walk down stairs; it has been shot into space, studied by NASA for its gravitational properties, and used as a makeshift antenna by soldiers in the Vietnam War.

IT'S NOT A BIRD, IT'S NOT A PLANE . . . IS IT BIAS?

Superman is the most popular superhero. Is this statement a fact, a bias, or a point of view? Read below to tell the difference …

Bias: An unbalanced opinion; a judgment based on a personal point of view. If your favorite superhero is Iron Man, you're probably biased in some way against other superheroes. You may think Iron Man's armor makes him stronger than Superman, and you may try to convince non–Iron Man fans that the weapons he invented are superior. You may even argue that his genius makes him better than all the Avengers put together!

Bias often creeps up in everyday life when people talk about the things they like, be that music, sports, books, or movies. Bias can be detected in all sorts of information resources, including primary and secondary sources.

- ☆ **Primary sources:** Written or spoken accounts of events created within the time frame being investigated. Primary sources provide firsthand information about an event, person, or place, and can include letters, blogs, diaries, photographs, podcasts, advertisements, interviews, and films.
- ☆ **Secondary sources:** Sources that analyze, restate, or explain primary sources. For example, encyclopedias, textbooks, books, magazines, articles, and websites can all be secondary sources.

Fact: An objective statement that can be verified in other sources. For example: *The War of 1812 officially began on June 18, 1812, when the United States signed a declaration of war against Britain.* This historical fact is easily verified across different sources.

Point of View: A statement, or opinion, based on personal belief. Just who exactly won the War of 1812 is debatable. Well-respected historians on both sides have different opinions on the subject: some gather facts to support their belief that the Americans won, while others present evidence that Canada was the real victor of the war. Don't assume everything you read, even from credible sources, is fact: check out multiple sources to help form your argument.

The three Ws (on the next page) will help you recognize bias and spot the difference between fact and point of view.

Evaluating Sources with the Three Ws

Like superheroes who never leave home without putting on their nifty disguises, super-learners won't embark on a learning mission before consulting the three Ws: Who, When, and Why. This powerful trio will arm you to judge the reliability of your sources. Think of the three Ws as your super-learner sidekick spies, here to help you detect false information during your research.

Who

Can you trust the author of that document you're reading?

☆ The final part of a website's address (the URL) will tell you something about who's providing the information. For example: the .com extension is used by commercial companies; .org, by nonprofits (organizations that exist to achieve specific goals, instead of existing for the purpose of making a profit); .gov by US government websites; and .edu by educational institutions. Different countries also have different site endings: .ca is used for Canadian websites, .fr for France, and .br for Brazil, just to name a few.

☆ Track down some reviews to see what others have thought of the author's work in the past.

Is he or she considered an expert on the subject, and if so, by whom?

☆ If the author's name comes up in other reliable or respected sources while you're doing your research, that's usually a good sign! If the author is influential in the field, and has a lot of writing to show for it, he or she is more likely to be trustworthy.

When
Is the information up-to-date?
☆ For online sources, the date of last update is usually found at the bottom of a webpage. The publication date of most print sources is usually found at the beginning of a book or an article.

Does it need to be current?
☆ It's important that scientific, medical, and technological information be up-to-date because change is frequent in these fields. In the fields of history or philosophy, however, the oldest works can often be the most authoritative.

Why
Why has the author created this work?
☆ A news article is meant to inform and explain the facts objectively, whereas an editorial aims to persuade the reader of the author's opinion on a particular subject.
☆ All information sources, even reliable ones, have a point of view and a bias. As a super-learner, it's your mission to consider both.

ARE YOU A CRITICAL THINKER?

How critical are you when it comes to thinking about the world? Take this quiz and find out!

Q1 When watching a scary movie, you're more likely to think about
a) how the director used sound effects and music to heighten the suspense
b) whether or not there's going to be a sequel

Q2 When reading a book, you're probably wondering
a) if the author's choice of setting was informed by his own personal experiences
b) if you can get your hands on the movie version

Q3 When deciding which chocolate bar to purchase, you usually look for
a) an official fair trade certification logo
b) the least expensive option

Q4 If you were offered two jobs at the same time, how would you decide which was the best employer to work for?
a) speak to people who have worked there, watch the news to see if the companies have been mentioned and how, and research their history
b) check out each company's Facebook page to see how many people "like" them online

Q5 Which website will provide the most objective information about buying the latest gaming system?

a) a website that publishes reviews and comparisons of consumer products

b) the game company's own website

Q6 When making an important decision, what are you more likely to do?

a) rely upon my own intuition, common sense, and past experience

b) create a social media post to take friends' reactions and opinions into account

Q7 Before getting a dog, what are you most likely to consider?

a) what kind of dog is best suited to my family, given our lifestyle and housing situation

b) the types of things I want to do with the dog, like going hiking, taking her to the beach, and going to the dog park

It's time to tally up your score! If you got mostly As, your powers of critical thinking are right on track—"more powerful than a locomotive," in Superman terms. If you got more Bs, you might need to don your critical-thinking cape. Check out the section on the next page to see what it all means.

To Be or Not to Be
A Critical Thinker

A critical thinker is someone who evaluates information based on its credibility and accuracy, and approaches problems aware of his or her own thoughts, beliefs, and viewpoints, as well as those of others.

Super-learners are not only armed with accurate information and equipped to think critically, they also avoid making assumptions at all costs. An assumption is an idea based on too little, or unreliable, information. Harnessing your powers of critical thinking leads to solutions that are both rational and fair. Just like superheroes searching for truth and justice, critical thinkers are willing to explore, question, and seek answers for themselves.

YOUR DIGITAL SUPERPOWER: INFORMATION LITERACY

If super-learners are the superheroes of the real world, then information literacy is the superpower for our digital age. As a super-learner, one of your greatest challenges is to critically evaluate information in the modern world, a place where choices about what to listen to, read, or watch can be overwhelming.

The ability to recognize bias and to take it into account when making decisions is a heroic task. It will serve you well both inside the classroom and on other epic adventures, in this world and beyond.

You've prepared your lair, accepted your mission, and vanquished a villain or two along the way. Now it's time to tackle the digital world: a world full of peril and possibility.

Chapter 4

TO THE INTERNET AND BEYOND!

DISCOVER NEW WORLDS

Ah, webs—Spidey's amazing superpower … Bet you didn't know you can spin one, too, and with just the touch of a finger (or two)? This web, the Internet, is a truly awesome resource for learning that can take you to some amazing places! No matter how old you are or where you come from, the Internet allows you to share your ideas, connect with all kinds of people, and communicate with friends and family around the world.

This incredible superpower—the ability to surf the web—is usually free and can be used anytime an Internet connection is available.

In this chapter, you will discover the secrets of smart digital citizens. The web, if used wisely, will help you become a successful super-learner. But don't get caught in it! Staying safe and being respectful is the key to harnessing the awesome power of the Internet.

ARE YOU INTERNET SAVVY?

Sure, the web can take you places faster than The Flash, but be smart and make sure you know where you are going. Take this quiz to find out whether you're a responsible digital citizen.

Q1 **While in an online chat room, another user asks you for your name and the name of your school. You've never encountered this user before. How does this make you feel?**
a) I feel excited to be making a new friend.
b) It makes me feel uneasy. I would report this request to a trusted adult right away.

Q2 **Which pieces of information should not be shared online?**
a) my pet's name, my favorite movie, and the last place I went on vacation
b) my name, my email address, and my phone number

Q3 **You get an email from a person you've never heard of before congratulating you for winning a free iPad. What would you do?**
a) update my social media status letting everyone know what just happened
b) delete the email right away, without replying to it

Q4 Your book report is due tomorrow morning and you haven't started working on it yet. What would you do?

  a) copy and paste sections of a book review I found online into my report and call it a night
  b) take a deep breath and relax—I've got a busy night ahead of me!

Q5 You're thinking about buying a new skateboard. To figure out which company is best, would you read

  a) a review of the skateboard posted on the company's website?
  b) a review of all kinds of skateboards, posted on a consumer website?

Q6 What would you do if someone tagged you in a nasty message?

  a) I'd write a response defending myself.
  b) I would ignore the comments and resist the urge to fight back online, and then talk to someone I trust about how the post made me feel.

Q7 You pass by a computer at school and see that a classmate has left her email account open by mistake. What would you do?

a) read through all her emails to see if she's said anything about me or my friends

b) log out of her email right away, find her, and let her know she'd accidentally left her account open and that you closed it for her.

Q8 What is a chat room moderator or monitor?

a) a gadget that makes sure a chat room stays open. All online chat rooms must have a moderator.

b) someone who watches what people are saying in a chat room and has the ability to kick people out for rude or inappropriate comments. Only certain chat rooms have moderators.

It's time to tally up your score! If you got mostly As, you still have some stuff to learn about acting responsibly and safely online. If you got mostly Bs, then congratulations—your Internet know-how is right on track. A combination of As and Bs means you're somewhere in the middle.

Protecting Yourself Online

Want to learn more about how to protect yourself and your identity online? Check out these sites:

Toronto Public Library KidsSpace
www.tpl.ca/kids/online-safety
This site has quizzes, links, and other useful information that will help you stay safe online.

Media Smarts
www.mediasmarts.ca
With information about digital and media literacy for you, your parents, and teachers, this site has something for everyone.

CyberQuoll
www.cybersmart.gov.au
The cyber safety tips and advice on this Australian website are entertaining and useful. A must-read for all super-learners.

Every Superhero Needs A Sidekick

One of the greatest and most challenging things about digital information is that it's so easy to create and share.

* You can take, upload, and share a photo with just a few clicks.
* You can create a public website or blog in minutes about absolutely anything you feel like writing about.
* You can share files with anyone with an Internet connection anywhere in the world.

Digital information is also really easy to copy. But just because you have the power to copy and paste, doesn't mean it's right. To become a true super-learner, you'll have to get there honestly. Like any superhero, you will face obstacles and huge amounts of pressure. You can't always do it alone! Turn to a trusty sidekick, a friend who can remind you that it is important to respect creative work you find online.

Plagiarism: Passing off someone else's work as if it were your own. Plagiarism originally comes from a Latin word that means

kidnapper—a villain, which all superheroes are equipped to fight!

You've already encountered some of the ways to combat plagiarism in the previous chapters. Managing your time and learning how to take proper notes goes a long way to ensuring that you give credit where it is due.

Copyright: A law that protects creators' rights to their work. Just because you find something online, doesn't make it yours to do with as you please—everyone is responsible for following copyright laws, both online and in the real world.

Creative Commons License: A legal notice attached to online content that lets you know it can be used and shared. A license like this tells you how you can use a particular work, whether it's a photo, video, sound bite, or a piece of writing. The license may allow you to copy, distribute, and display the content freely no matter what the purpose, or it may limit its use to noncommercial purposes only.

When completing assignments or just hanging out online, be thoughtful about how you copy and paste. If you use any-one else's content or images, be sure to credit them and add the source to a list of references (a shout-out also works!). Give them some link-love by pointing other users to their site, if they have one.

THE INTERNET: THE GOOD, THE BAD, AND THE UGLY

Chapter 3 showed you how to evaluate sources to make sure they're credible and gave you tips to be super-bias-detectors. But wait! Bias is everywhere, not just in research resources. It's also tied up in your everyday web experience. Don't get trapped!

Search engines work with algorithms—mathematical calculations—to help web browsers get you where you want to go. These calculations themselves can be biased.

Advertising: Commercials aren't just for TV anymore. Advertisers also have a powerful, but not always obvious, presence online. Every one of your actions, from where and what you search to the content you post, has potential commercial value to companies.

* Sponsored links often show up first when you search. These advertisements may look like all the other links in your hit list (the results of your search), but they are actually ads about products and services related specifically to the keywords you used. Their goal is to get you to click on them first. For example, if you were searching for the best milk shake in your area, sponsored links for ice cream companies might appear at the very top of your hit list, before actual reviews about milk shakes.
* Advertisers also help pay the costs of running free online applications. Facebook, for example, is a great way to connect with friends. It's also a very effective way for advertisers to connect with you. Watch out for ads placed on your profile page and newsfeed.

Customization: To alter something to meet individual characteristics. You've probably figured out that you can customize some computer games yourself, like Minecraft. But did you know that the Internet will customize some things for you, whether or not you ask for it? You have to be savvy to spot this sneaky cyber superpower. It's the work of those stealth algorithms again …

* Have you ever noticed that a search engine sometimes knows what kind of search you want to do, even before you've finished typing? Your keyword search has been customized to suggest the most popular searches, your most common searches, and searches based on where you are located.
* Personal information you've shared in the past can be used to craft a particular view of a subject. If you've

ever shopped for books online, for example, your past choices help to inform the searches you've yet to perform in the future (talk about sci-fi algorithms!). If you search for a bunch of books about dogs, the next time you look for books on animals, dogs will be front-and-center in the suggestions you receive. This can also mean that on websites you visit, you start to notice ads that are targeted toward your personal interests. This can be very enticing, and also very intrusive since you're never asked if you want to see these kinds of ads or not.

Next time you're searching for information online, remember to balance your cyber-finds with information found in the physical world as well:

☆ Check out print sources, at school, at a library, or at home. Remember, not everything can be found online. The library is a great place to search for these very valuable sources.
☆ Seek out the advice of a librarian or a teacher. They'll have suggestions on where to look for the information you need.
☆ Look to experts in the field you're investigating for another point of view.
☆ Talk to family and friends about resources they find useful.

Don't forget about inappropriate and illegal content. Keep super-vigilant for these villains:

Scams and hoaxes: Tricks to make you believe in something that is not true. Be careful not to open emails from people or businesses you don't know. Bogus emails can contain all kinds of nasty things as attachments: computer viruses or illegal and offensive pictures and movie files.

Phishing: A particular form of online scam in which you receive a fake cry for help. The perpetrator tries to get at your most private information by sharing a sob story, like being stranded in a foreign country, or needing quick medical aid, in the hopes that you'll feel sorry and take action. A message like this might come from a familiar-looking email address, so beware!

Cyberbullying: Using technology, like a cell phone or a computer, to deliberately upset someone else. Internet trolls are people who set out to start arguments online—a form of online harassment. Examples of cyberbullying can also include
☆ nasty messages or threats sent via email
☆ insults posted on a social networking site or other public website
☆ gossiping about someone in a chat room or over an instant messenger
☆ inappropriate photos or videos sent or shared
Like superheroes, super-learners defend others, online as well as in the real world. Help vanquish the trolls and bullies by refusing to look at or forward harassing messages or images. Take action! Report the problem to a trusted adult.

Downloading: To transfer content, like movies, music, or software, to your computer. But beware! On top of breaking copyright laws, using illegal file-sharing programs can put you and your computer in harm's way. When you download pirated software, you may end up with more than just the files you intended; you may also expose yourself to spyware, viruses, and other nasty things that can compromise your privacy and safety. Content that is pirated is illegally down-loaded. If you like the artist you're listening to, or watching, support them by purchasing their music or movies on a legal site.

Just like places in the real world that you might not want to visit (think scary or inappropriate), there are also places to stay away from online. Wherever your learning adventure takes you in the digital world, make sure you feel safe and comfortable.

For more information about online nasties and other terms, check out the glossary at the end of this book (page 66).

Digital Cartographers: Super-Learners in Your Midst

Youth around the world are using maps to accomplish their goals and make changes for the better in their communities.

Salim Shekh and Sikha Patra were surprised to learn that their community in India—a Calcutta slum—did not appear on Google Maps. With the help of their teacher, Amlan Ganguly, they set out to create the neighborhood's first map.

This map helped them to organize community events, including a polio vaccination campaign. Using cell phones, Salim and Sikha went door to door collecting data about which children needed to be immunized against polio and where they lived. Their text messages were instantaneously uploaded into a database that was linked to a digital online community map, showing exactly where they needed to focus outreach for the vaccination campaign.

A couple of American filmmakers captured their story in the documentary *The Revolutionary Optimists*. The film inspired BAVC (Bay Area Video Coalition) Producers Institute for New Technologies to develop Map Your World (http://revolutionaryoptimists.org), a web-based tool that enables kids to use mobile technologies to improve health in their communities.

Salim and Sikha proved that high-tech gadgets aren't just the domain of superheroes. With the help of Map Your World, Salim and Sikha were better able to help their community fight for the things it needed. It might not be as glitzy as a batsuit, a teleportation machine, or a cosmic hover board, but mapping software can be just as revolutionary.

In Oakland, California, students use mapping software to track cigarette litter to better understand how it impacts their city, while students in Florida track bear sightings to promote bear awareness amongst their neighbors. How could you use mapping software in your own community to help change things for the better?

THINK BEFORE YOU POST

Have you ever noticed how you communicate online? Is it different from your dealings in the real world? Sometimes it's easier to say things online that you wouldn't feel comfortable saying in a face-to-face situation, but does that make it right? After all, the Internet really is just another place, and the same rules should apply.

Hurtful information posted online may be difficult to remove and can be seen by a whole bunch of people. Publishing anything unkind or rude can lead to flame wars—heated arguments between individuals. Be careful what you put on the Internet; when it's published, it's out there for everyone to see and possibly misinterpret or misuse. And it's very hard to take back.

Netiquette = Etiquette + the Internet

Below are some rules that smart digital citizens should consider when practicing netiquette:

* ☆ Don't say anything to someone online that you wouldn't say face-to-face.
* ☆ Remember Internet copyright and make sure you have permission to post the things you do.
* ☆ Keep flame wars under control.
* ☆ Respect other people's privacy.
* ☆ Write in lowercase letters (CAPITALS EQUAL SHOUTING!!!!)

How to Use the Internet Responsibly

Internet safety is more than just a set of rules. It's about understanding how to avoid problems like being hurt, ripped off, bullied, scammed, or stalked. No one wants to deal with that while they're trying to have a good time online.

Melvil Dewey and the Caveman

In 1876, when super-learner Melvil Dewey (librarian, educator, and inventor of the Dewey Decimal System) was asked to reorganize the collections of a library in which he worked, he thought back … way, way back.

He asked himself: What would a primitive man wonder about the world around him? His imagination produced the following questions, which helped to shape the still–widely used Dewey Decimal System.

Who Am I?
✰ Encyclopedia and world records, philosophy and psychology (100s)

What Is Greater than Me?
✰ Astrology and the supernatural, world religions (200s)

Who Is Like Me?
✰ Holidays, folk and fairy tales, scary stories, law and governments (300s)

How Do We Communicate?
✰ Dictionaries and languages (400s)

What Is the Natural World?
✰ Math, stars and planets, electricity and magnets, chemistry, earthquakes and volcanoes, weather, rocks and minerals, dinosaurs, plants, bugs, fish and amphibians, birds, mammals (500s)

How Do I Use the Natural World?
☆ Inventions, the human body, pets, cooking and food (600s)

What Cool Things Can I Do in My Spare Time?
☆ Drawing and cartoons, crafts, art, music, sports (700s)

How Can I Express My Ideas?
☆ Poetry, plays, jokes and riddles (800s)

How Can I Find Out about Other Places and Times?
☆ Explorers and atlases, ancient civilizations, countries, knights and castles (900s)

Cyber Glossary

Attachment: A photo, music, or text file included with a message sent online.

Browser: Software that allows you to see and connect to sites on the web.

Chat room: A place to go online where you can talk with people who have similar interests to yours.

Cyberbullying: The use of technology such as computers and cell phones to deliberately upset someone. Cyberbullying is usually a repeated behavior.

File sharing: The act of searching for and copying music, movies, and files from other people's computers to your own.

Flaming: An insulting interaction between Internet users. Also known as flame wars, flaming tends to happen in unmoderated chat rooms.

Internet: The network of computers connected worldwide via telephone wires, cables, and satellites.

Moderator: The person who is responsible for ensuring that nothing bad happens in an online chat room.

Netiquette: Guidelines for polite and considerate behavior online.

Phishing: An online scam whereby people posing as legitimate organizations or individuals send misleading email requests for personal and financial details.

Privacy settings: A social networking tool that will help you stay in control of your privacy. A privacy policy tells you how a website can use your personal information.

Spam: Emails, or instant messages, usually of a commercial nature, that you never signed up to receive.

Spyware: A computer program installed on personal computers, usually without consent, that collects personal information.

Trolling: The posting of inflammatory comments. Trolls seek to gain attention by disrupting a conversation in an online community such as a chat room, forum, or blog. This can be a one-time occurrence.

Username: An online nickname used to protect your real name and identity. Also known as a handle.

Virus: A program written with the intent of damaging a computer's operations. Viruses can spread between computers, infecting more than just one. Computers can be protected against viruses by anti-virus software.

World Wide Web: The part of the Internet that houses webpages, linked to one another around the world.

Sources

Chapter 1

American Library Association Presidential Committee on Information Literacy: Final Report. Chicago: American Library Association, 1989. Web. 15 May 2014.

Discover Your Preferred Learning Style. *Brainboxx.* John Fewings, n.d. Web. 21 May 2014.

Dodgson, Rose, and Tim Gauntley. *Imagine the Learning!: Elementary Research Success @ Your Library: A Guide for Elementary Teacher-Librarians and Teachers to Use with Students.* Toronto: Toronto District School Board, 2006. Print.

"On Pi Day, Finding Strength in Numbers." *CNN Wire*, March 14, 2014 pNA. Infotrac Junior Edition. Web. 6 June 2014.

Chapter 2

Booth, Wayne C. Gregory G. Colomb, and Joseph M. Williams. *The Craft of Research,* 3rd ed. Chicago: University of Chicago Press, 2008. Print.

"Malala Yousafzai." *Gale Biography in Context.* Detroit: Gale, 2012. Biography in Context. Web. 12 June 2014.

Ogle, D.M. "K-W-L: A Teaching Model that Develops Active Reading of Expository Text." *The Reading Teacher*, Vol. 39, No. 6 (1989), 564–70. Print.

Toronto Public Library. *The Research Virtuoso: How to Find Anything You Need to Know*. Toronto: Annick Press, 2012. Print.

Chapter 3

"Alexander Fleming." Britannica School. Encyclopædia Britannica, Inc., 2014. Web. 5 August 2014.

"Betty and Richard James." *Business Leader Profiles for Students.* Ed. Sheila Dow and Jaime E. Noce, eds. Vol. 2. Detroit: Gale, 2002. Biography in Context. Web. 4 June 2014.

Booth, Wayne C. Gregory G. Colomb, and Joseph M. Williams. *The Craft of Research,* 3rd ed. Chicago: University of Chicago Press, 2008. Print.

"Chris Hadfield." *Gale Biography in Context.* Detroit: Gale, 2013. Biography in Context. Web. 14 August 2014.

Dodgson, Rose, and Tim Gauntley. *Imagine the Learning!: Elementary Research Success @ Your Library: A Guide for Elementary Teacher-Librarians and Teachers to Use with Students*. Toronto,: Toronto District School Board, 2006. Print.

Ruth H. Rockwood. "Melvil Dewey and Librarianship." *The Journal of Library History (1966–1972)*, Vol. 3, No. 4 (Oct. 1968), pp. 329–341. Print.

Starkey, Lauren B. *Critical Thinking Skills Success in 20 Minutes a Day*. New York, NY: LearningExpress, 2010. Print.

Toronto Public Library. *The Research Virtuoso: How to Find Anything You Need to Know*. Toronto: Annick Press, 2012. Print.
Wales, Andrew. "The Happy Accident." *Hopscotch*. Vol. 21, Issue 3 (Oct.–Nov. 2009), p. 24. General Reference Center GOLD. Web. 4 June 2014.

"War of 1812." Britannica School. Encyclopædia Britannica, Inc., 2014. Web. 9 July 2014.

Chapter 4

Common Sense Media. Common Sense Media Advocacy Group, 2003. Web. 7 July 2014. www.commonsensemedia.org/.

CyberQuoll—Internet Safety Education for Primary School Students, Parents Guide. Australian Communications and Media Authority, 2009. Web. 7 July 2014. www.cybersmart.gov.au/cyberquoll/resources/parents/cyberquoll_parentsguide.pdf.

Google company overview. Web. 25 June 2014. www.google.ca/intl/en/about/company/.

Head, Alison J, and John Wihbey. "At Sea in Deluge of Data." *The Chronicle of Higher Education*, Vol. 61, No. 40 (2014). Web. 25 July 2014.

Internet safety for teens. *LookBothWays Inc*. Washington State Office of the Attorney General, 2008. Web. 7 July 2014. www.atg.wa.gov/InternetSafety/Teens.aspx.

Jane Goodall's Roots & Shoots. Web. 11 September 2014. www.rootsand-shoots.org/mapping.

KidsSpace. Kids@Computers Challenge. Toronto Public Library, 2008. Web. 7 July 2014. http://kidsspace.torontopubliclibrary.ca/kac_challenge.html.

Merry, Stephanie. "The Revolutionary Optimists: In India, Reason to Believe." *Washington Post*, 3 April 2013. *Academic OneFile*. Web. 25 June 2014.

Acknowledgments

This book is for learners of all stripes—those who feel like superheroes and those still trying to find their way. Anyone can become a superbrain; all you need are the right tools, curiosity, a willingness to learn, and some good old-fashioned encouragement. We hope that this book will help all budding superheroes in their quests for knowledge, furnishing them with the power of seeing the possible all around.

Thank-you to Emilia, a super-learner in training, for exemplifying just how magical donning a dish towel cape can be, and thank-you to all the kids out there (big and small) who revel in the joy of discovery that learning and imagination bring.